www.ingramcontent.com/pod-product-compliance
Lightning Source LLC
LaVergne TN
LVHW072051060526
838200LV00061B/4716

قاموسُ الصُّوَرِ الأوَّلُ
الحَيَوَاناتُ
First Picture Dictionary
Animals

فَراشَةٌ
Butterfly

خِنزيرٌ
Pig

ثَعلَبٌ
Fox

أرنَبٌ
Rabbit

الرسوم مِن قِبَل آنا إيفانير

www.kidkiddos.com
Copyright ©2025 by KidKiddos Books Ltd.
support@kidkiddos.com

All rights reserved. No part of this book may be reproduced in any form or by any electronic or mechanical means, including information storage and retrieval systems, without written permission from the publisher, except in the case of a reviewer, who may quote brief passages embodied in critical articles or in a review.
First edition, 2025

Library and Archives Canada Cataloguing in Publication
First Picture Dictionary - Animals (Arabic English Bilingual edition)
ISBN: 978-1-83416-273-7 paperback
ISBN: 978-1-83416-274-4 hardcover
ISBN: 978-1-83416-272-0 eBook

الحَيَواناتُ البَرِّيةُ
Wild Animals

أَسَدٌ
Lion

نَمِرٌ
Tiger

زَرافَةٌ
Giraffe

♦ الزَّرافَةُ هِيَ أَطوَلُ حَيَوانٍ عَلَى اليابِسَةِ.

♦ A giraffe is the tallest animal on land.

فِيلٌ
Elephant

قِردٌ
Monkey

أيَّل
Moose

ذِئبٌ
Wolf

♦ الأيَّلُ سَبّاحٌ ماهِرٌ ويَغوصُ تَحتَ الماءِ لِيَأكُلَ النَّباتاتِ!

♦ A moose is a great swimmer and can dive underwater to eat plants!

سِنجابٌ
Squirrel

كُوالا
Koala

♦ يُخَبِّئُ السِّنجابُ الجَوزَ لِلشِّتاءِ، وَلَكِنَّهُ أحيانًا يَنسى أينَ وَضَعَهُ!

♦ A squirrel hides nuts for winter, but sometimes forgets where it put them!

غُوريلّا
Gorilla

الحَيَواناتُ البَرِّيَّةُ
Wild Animals

قَرَسُ النَّهرِ
Hippopotamus

باندا
Panda

ثَعلَبٌ
Fox

وَحِيدُ القَرنِ
Rhino

غَزالٌ
Deer

سَمَكَةٌ ذَهَبِيَّةٌ
Goldfish

كَلْبٌ
Dog

◆ بَعْضُ البَبَّغاواتِ يُمكِنُها تَقليدُ الكَلِماتِ وَالضَّحِكُ مِثلَ الإِنسانِ!

◆ *Some parrots can copy words and even laugh like a human!*

قِطٌّ
Cat

بَبَّغاءٌ
Parrot

الحَيَواناتُ الأَليفَةُ
Pets

كَناريٌّ
Canary

✦ يَستَطيعُ الضِّفدَعُ أَن يَتَنَفَّسَ مِن جِلدِهِ وَرِئَتَيهِ!
✦ A frog can breathe through its skin as well as its lungs!

خنزير غينيا
Guinea Pig

ضِفدَعٌ
Frog

هامِستَر
Hamster

حَيواناتُ المَزرعَةِ
Animals at the Farm

بَقَرَةٌ
Cow

دَجاجَةٌ
Chicken

بَطَّةٌ
Duck

خَروفٌ
Sheep

حِصانٌ
Horse

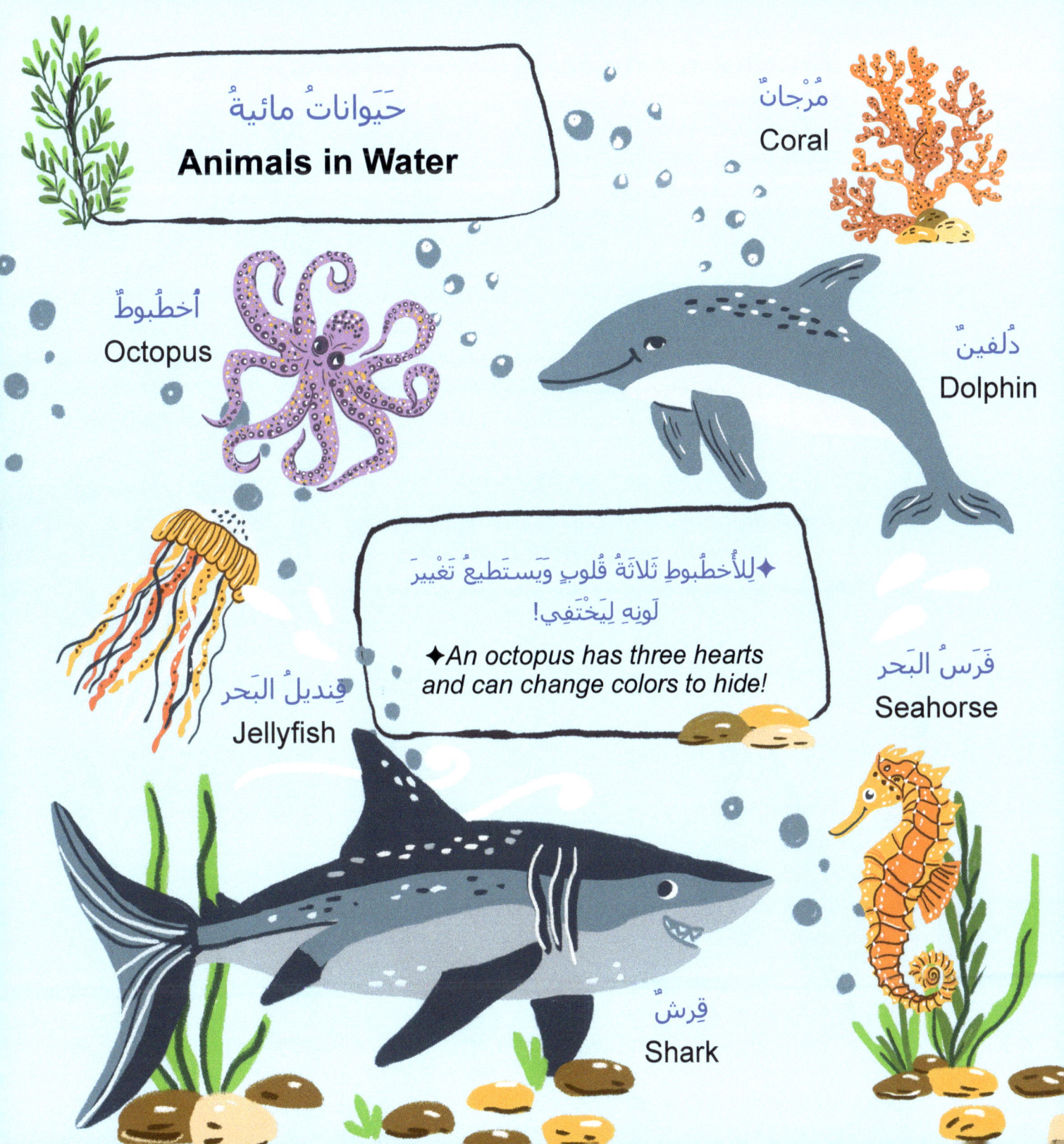

حَيَوَانَات سِحْرِيَّة
Magical Animals

وَحِيد القَرْن
Unicorn

بيغاسوس
Pegasus

تِنِّين
Dragon

حُورِيَّة البَحْر
Mermaid

حَيَوانَات صَغِيرَة
Small Animals

حَرْباء
Chameleon

عَنْكَبُوت
Spider

✦ النَّعَامَة أَكْبَر طَائِر، وَلَكِنَّها لَا تَسْتَطِيع الطَّيَرَان!
✦ *An ostrich is the biggest bird, but it cannot fly!*

نحْلَة
Bee

✦ يَحْمِل الحَلَزُون بَيْتَهُ عَلَى ظَهْرِهِ ويَتَحَرَّك بِبُطْء شَدِيد.
✦ *A snail carries its home on its back and moves very slowly.*

حَلَزُون
Snail

فَأر
Mouse

بومةٌ
Owl

خُفَّاشٌ
Bat

♦ تَصْطَادُ الْبُومَةُ لَيْلًا وَتَسْتَخْدِمُ سَمْعَهَا لِتَجِدَ الطَّعَامَ!

♦An owl hunts at night and uses its hearing to find food!

♦ تَتَوَهَّجُ الْيَرَقَانَةُ لِتَجِدَ آخَرِينَ مِنْ نَوْعِهَا.

♦A firefly glows at night to find other fireflies.

رَاكُونٌ
Raccoon

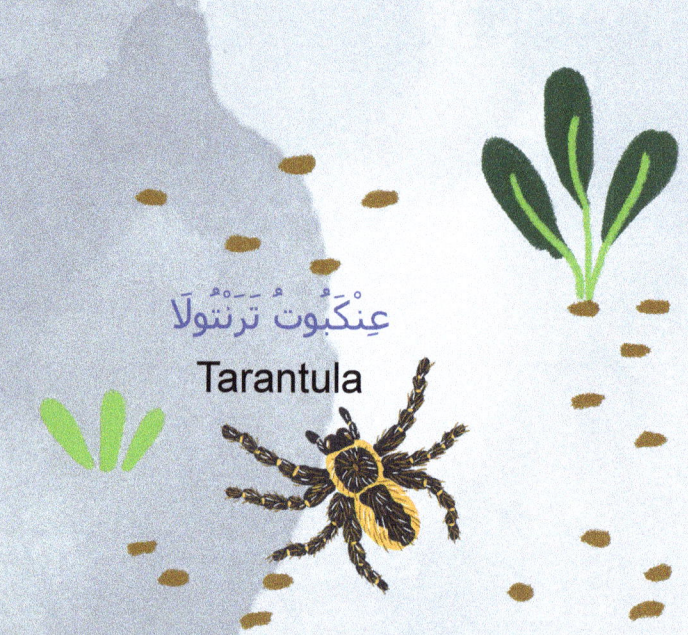

عِنْكَبُوتُ تَرَنْتُولَا
Tarantula

اَلْحَيَوَانَاتُ اللَّيْلِيَّةُ
Nighttime Animals

يَرَقَانَةٌ
Firefly

غَرِيرٌ
Badger

طَائِرُ الْكِيْوِي
Kiwi Bird

نَمِرٌ إفريقي
Leopard

قُنْفُذٌ
Hedgehog

اَلْحَيَوَانَاتُ الْمُلَوَّنَةُ
Colorful Animals

اَلْبُومَةُ لَوْنُهَا بُنِّيٌّ
An owl is brown

اَلْفْلَامِنْغُو لَوْنُهُ وَرْدِيٌّ
A flamingo is pink

اَلْبَجَعَةُ لَوْنُهَا أَبْيَضُ
A swan is white

اَلْأُخْطُبُوطُ لَوْنُهُ أُرْجُوَانِيٌّ
An octopus is purple

الضفدع لونه أخضر
A frog is green

◆ الضَّفْدَعُ أَخْضَرُ اللَّوْنِ لِيَسْتَطِيعَ الِاخْتِبَاءَ بَيْنَ الْأَوْرَاقِ.

◆ A frog is green, so it can hide among the leaves.

فَرَاشَةٌ وَيَرْقَانَةٌ
Butterfly and Caterpillar

خَرُوفٌ وَحَمَلٌ
Sheep and Lamb

حِصَانٌ وَمُهْرٌ
Horse and Foal

خِنْزِيرٌ وَخِنْزِيرٌ صَغِيرٌ
Pig and Piglet

مَاعِزٌ وَجَدْيٌ
Goat and Kid

اَلْحَيَوَانَاتُ وَصِغَارُهَا
Animals and Their Babies

بَقَرَةٌ وَعِجْلٌ
Cow and Calf

قِطَّةٌ وهِرَّة
Cat and Kitten

الدجاجة والكتكوت
Chicken and Chick

✦ الكَتْكُوت يُخَاطِبُ أُمَّهُ حَتَّى قَبْلَ أَنْ يَفْقِسَ.
✦ *A chick talks to its mother even before it hatches.*

كَلْبٌ وَجَرْوٌ
Dog and Puppy